Putting Your Angels To Work

Michael O. Amamieye
PUTTING Your
ANGELS
To Work

Unless otherwise indicated, all scripture quotations are from the King James Version of the Bible.

Copyrights © 2005, Michael O. Amamieye

Reprinted in 2011, 2020.

Published by:

Michael Amamieye Word Outreach, International

a/k/a Aggressive Faith Ministries

Plot 13 Walter Akpana Lay Out

Off 394 Ikwerre Road Mile 5 Rumueprikom

P. O. Box 12378, Port Harcourt, Nigeria.

E-mail: info@aggressivefaith.org

Web site: www.aggressivefaith.org

Phone: +2349018006296, +2348050987377

+2348036732188 (WhatsApp)

+1-916-245-6157 (U.S.A.)

ISBN: 978-978-35362-9-6

Printed in the Federal Republic of Nigeria

Putting Your Angels To Work

DEDICATION

I dedicate this book to the special angels God has planted in my life. They are so numerous that if I mention names, I will leave out especially the ones that have been assigned to perform God's word in my present and future assignments.

CONTENTS

INTRODUCTION

I am always fascinated at the supernatural dimension of life that makes this life very interesting. Before I had an encounter with Christ, I was aware of the supernatural. I knew that there are real spirit beings around us that either help or hurt human events and happenings. I was aware of the fact that if I knew how to activate them, I could use their powers to my advantage. I knew people use evil the support they mobilize from evil spirits otherwise called fallen angels to do a lot to their advantage.

"And it came to pass on the morrow, that the evil spirit from God came upon Saul, and he prophesied in the midst of the house: and David played with his hand, as at other times: and there was a javelin in Saul's hand.

11 And Saul cast the javelin; for he said, I will smite David even to the wall with it. And David avoided out of his presence twice."

1 Sam. 18:10-11.

Two things I want you to notice in the above scripture: one, evil spirits or fallen angels can move a man to prophesy or speak swelling words. Have you noticed men who speak with so much confidence as if they own the world? We used to observe them back in the eighties to be men and women who were in the occult. They were aided by some evil forces. They have certain emblems like rings they wear and then they make invocations and incantations that move these evil spirits to do their biddings. Before you dismiss that as nothing, find out the damage they caused.

Two, evil spirits or fallen angels can motivate a man to do extraordinary acts. Saul in his right mind could not have used that javelin to strike David. However, an evil spirit can blind the sensibilities of a man to do things that can be attributed to being under an influence that supersedes him.

Just as much as fallen angels still have these capacities, you can imagine what the good angels can do. The fact is that, anything the fallen angels can do in their fallen state, the good angels can do the direct opposite. The reason is that the fallen angels are in the opposite camp and they are wired to do anything and everything that is opposite God. They don't have the capacity or capability to do otherwise. Just the same way the good angels are wired to do good. They just can't do otherwise.

When you begin to discover for yourself the tremendous powers these angels wield and that you can activate them for your advantage, it will change the dynamics of life on earth. I don't need fallen angels because they are fallen. They have lost out on all they used to be and have. Just like every ex-president, these fallen angels don't have the kinds of capacity or capability they used to have unless man gives it to them.

"And he said unto them, I beheld Satan as lightning fall from heaven.

Behold, I give unto you power to tread on serpents and scorpions, and over all the power of the enemy: and nothing shall by any means hurt you.

Notwithstanding in this rejoice not, that the spirits are subject unto you; but rather rejoice, because your names are written in heaven."
Luke 10:18-20.

Take note of what Jesus said above: He supervised the fall of Satan and all fallen angels. They fell. They are no more what they used to be. They can't do what they used to. They don't have the abilities they used to.

As if that was not enough, Jesus turns to those who believe in Him and said, *I give you power*… You now have the power to do to these fallen angels what they can't stop or resist. Beyond that, Jesus said, that is not as important as the fact that your name is written in the book of life. Yes, these spirits both good and evil are subject to you, you can rejoice about that.

Jesus by implication is showing us that those whose names are written in heaven are above the good and evil spirits. In fact, the spirits are subject to them whose names are written in heaven. That He was addressing those who believed and followed Him means that for your name to be written in heaven, you have to believe in Him and follow Him. Wow!

"Also I say unto you, Whosoever shall confess me before men, him shall the Son of man also confess before the angels of God:

But he that denieth me before men shall be denied before the angels of God."

Luke 12:8-9.

If you are not sure if your name is written in heaven, all you need to do is to make this simple confession from your heart:

Lord Jesus, I believe that You are the Son of God. I am a sinner. You are my Savior. Come into my heart and be my Lord forever. I accept You Jesus Christ as the Lord of my life from this day in Jesus name. Amen.

Congratulations!

Putting Your Angels To Work

1

ANGELS ARE REAL

*"For he shall give his angels charge over thee,
to keep thee in all thy ways."*

Psalm 91:11.

*"Bless the LORD, ye his angels, that excel in
strength, that do his commandments,
hearkening unto the voice of his word."*

Psalm 103:20.

As a citizen of the world, I recognize my divine assignment here on earth. I am here on a special assignment as God's representative. I see myself as an Ambassador of the Most High God. Every ambassador must have the security and protection of his or her country in a strange and foreign land. His country will go to any extent to secure his or her provision and protection in a foreign land.

With this fact in mind, I submit that if human beings can make adequate provision and protection for their representatives in foreign nations, I believe that God who sent us on assignment on earth made adequate arrangement for our security from the time we arrive here on earth until we depart. Your supplies and security from the womb to the tomb has been secured with heavens guarantee. This is why He specially assigns angels to children.

"Take heed that ye despise not one of these little ones; for I say unto you, That in heaven their angels do always behold the face of my Father which is in heaven."

Matt. 18:10.

I do not know if these angels are assigned to every child born into this world or specifically for children born into the kingdom of God. The Scripture is not clear on this but from the above Scripture, Jesus was talking about children. If every child born into this world has an angel assigned to them, it becomes evident to me that when this child becomes born again, he or she is assigned more than one angel. That is to say that he or she has an additional angel to the one assigned by God from childhood. I also believe that some are assigned an angel or more depending on what they have been designed to accomplish on earth.

"Are they not all ministering spirits, sent forth to minister for them who shall be heirs of salvation?"

Heb. 1:14.

These angelic beings are spirits specially sent by God to rescue, deliver, and supply, to those who are heirs or inheritors of God's kingdom. In fact, they are sent even before they become heirs. As you would see later, they are responsible for guiding the steps of several to the place where the gospel was able to reach them that eventually brought about their salvation or deliverance or rescue.

I remember one time when I got into London, it was still snowing. I don't like snow at all and that is one reason why I don't travel to anywhere in the world when it is winter. It would take a special miracle from God for me to travel during winter. On this trip, I carried my luggage which were so heavy. The cold froze my hands to the point where I felt like my hands were detached from my body. I was agonizing inside. If you know England at all, nobody would normally go out of their way to help you. I needed help very much.

At one point, I just cried out to the Lord for help. I discovered that the shortest route to help is to cry out. The miracle took place. In less than one minute, I saw two sporty and smart young fellows walked up to me and asked me in their British accent if I needed help. I took a deep breath and screamed to let them know how much I needed help. That was how both of them shared my baggage and helped me to my destination.

I knew those were angels because it is not typical to get help from even your friends in Britain. I know that angels are real. I have seen them help me as I travel around the nations of the world fulfilling the great commission. They are here for you, to help you if you are born again. They have a charge, a command and a commission from God to keep you in all your ways. This commission puts a mandate on them to protect and preserve you as well as provide for your needs as long as you are on course.

The Hebrew and Greek words for angel mean the same thing. The Hebrew, *mal'ak* and Greek, *angelos* simply mean a messenger. It suggests an envoy with a commission to deliver a message as his primary function. Secondary functions include enforcing the message or serving the message with whatever it requires to make the message work.

Putting Your Angels To Work

2

NATURE OF ANGELS

There are two classes of angels. The good and the bad. The good ones are the ones that have kept their estate by obeying God's commands. The bad ones are ugly even though sometimes they still parade themselves with the same shine that they had before they were thrown out of heaven. However, they all have their origin in God. God created them for His pleasure and to fulfill His plans.

"Thou, even thou, art LORD alone; thou hast made heaven, the heaven of heavens, with all their host, the earth, and all things that are therein, the seas, and all that is therein, and

thou preservest them all; and the host of heaven worshippeth thee."

Neh. 9:6.

"For by him were all things created, that are in heaven, and that are in earth, visible and invisible, whether they be thrones, or dominions, or principalities, or powers: all things were created by him, and for him."

Col. 1:16.

"Thou art worthy, O Lord, to receive glory and honour and power: for thou hast created all things, and for thy pleasure they are and were created."

Rev. 4:11.

Satan is the head of the bad angels. They are also called demons. They became bad when they rebelled against God along with Lucifer.

"And the angels which kept not their first estate, but left their own habitation, he hath reserved in everlasting chains under darkness unto the judgment of the great day."

Jude 6.

Their eternal abode is in hell. It was for them that God created hell. ***"...everlasting fire, prepared for the devil and his demons."*** Matt. 25:41. Satan and his demons lost their place in heaven, their first estate and as a result, they became dysfunctional and disabled. As bad as they are, God still uses them to fulfill His purpose on earth. 1 Sam. 16:14,23. 18:10. 19:9. 1 Kings 22.

Angels are spirit beings. They are not flesh and blood. However, they can take the forms and fashion of human personalities, beings and objects. Zech. 6:5. Heb. 1:14. Eph. 6:12.

From the Hebrew definition of angels, there are three categories of angels you need to know. I believe the Hebrew expression helps us put a distinction in all angelic beings. The Hebrew word, *mal'ak*, tells us that these groups of angels are messengers. I call them **WAITING ANGELS**. They are like waiters. They wait on God's instructions to be carried out and enforced. They are *ministering angels* or *spirits*. They are all serving God's purpose. From the Bible, it looks like Gabriel is the chief waiting angel as we see him deliver God's messages severally in both Old and New Testaments. Dan. 8:15-19. 9:20-23. Luke 1:19.

The Hebrew *tseba'ot* which has a Greek equivalent, *sabaoth*, is translated most times as hosts or armies. These angelic beings are what I call **WARRING ANGELS**. The Hebrew and Greek word connotes an army of rest. They are a host of soldiers with a commission to enforce peace. These angels constitute God's peace keeping force. They are God's military might. They fight in battles at God's order and command. Michael seem to be the chief warring angel as we see in the Bible. Dan. 10:13,21. Jude 9. Rev. 12:7.

Apart from the two words above, there is this Hebrew word, *sharath*, used for angels. It is translated as minister or servant or worshiper. I call these angels **WORSHIP ANGELS**. All angels fall into this group because their primary assignment is to worship God. Lucifer was the chief worship angel before his fall. From the Bible, he was replaced with the twenty four elders or chiefs. Isa. 14:12. Rev. 4:10.

Putting Your Angels To Work

3

TWELVE THINGS YOU

SHOULD KNOW ABOUT ANGELS

One, they are spirits. They are called ministering or servant spirits. They were designed by God to serve Him and His purpose.

"Are not the angels all ministering spirits (servants) sent out in the service [of God for the assistance] of those who are to inherit salvation?"

Heb. 1:14. Amplified Version.

Two, they are called sons of God sometimes because they are extensions of God. They were created by God. They are members of the God kind of being. They can do what God commands them to do. Gen. 6:2,4. Job 1:6. 2:1.

Three, they were created long before mankind was created. They have been in existence long before the first man was created. Job 38:1-8.

Four, they have soul, that is the faculty to reason (mind), make decisions (will) and express feelings (emotions). Thus, you can reason with them. They can decide in keeping with God's plan for a person or place or position. Gen. 6:2. 18:1-5. Num. 22:22-35.

Five, they receive direct instructions from God. God and His word are the only instructors that move or motivate them to action. Judges 13:3,8,9. Matt. 26:52-53.

Six, they are very many and so they are not omnipresent. One cannot be in several places at the same time. Only God can. Angels are innumerable. Dan. 7:9,10. Luke 2:13. Heb. 12:22.

Seven, they are mighty in power even though they are not omnipotent or almighty. Only God is Omnipotent and Almighty. One angel can destroy an entire part or portion of the earth if commanded by God.

"Praise the Lord, you his angels, you mighty ones who do his bidding, who obey his word."

Psa. 103:20. New International Version.

Eight, they are very wise but not omniscient. Only God is Omniscient. Angels are not robots. They have the capacity to exercise the wisdom of God in carrying out their assignments. 2 Sam. 14:17,20. Matt. 24:36.

Nine, they are inferior to Christ by nature. They are not to be compared with Christ in any way or manner.

"So he has become much better than angels, and the name God has given him is superior to theirs."

Heb 1:4. Complete Jewish Bible.

In fact, they are lower in nature than man in his redeemed state. They were created to be lower than man in nature because man was made in the resemblance of God.

"And God said, Let us make man in our image, after our likeness..."

Gen. 1:26.

Redeemed man is in the same class with God.

"And He raised us up together with Him and made us sit down together [giving us joint seating with Him] in the heavenly sphere [by virtue of our being] in Christ Jesus (the Messiah, the Anointed One)."

Eph. 2:6. Amplified Version.

Ten, they are not to be worshiped. Nowhere in the entire Bible that the worship of angels is allowed. The worship of angels is idolatry. They were created by God to worship God and not to be worshipped at all. Judges 13:16. Col. 2:18. Rev. 19:10. 22:8-9.

Eleven, they have names and their names are a secret to God alone. There are only a few of them that we have their names revealed to us in the Bible. Other than these, their names are top secret to God. He calls them by name and sends them to serve specific purpose or person or place. Gen. 32:29. Judges 13:17-18.

Twelve, they can be entertained without you knowing that you have entertained an angel or angels.

"Do not forget or neglect or refuse to extend hospitality to strangers [in the brotherhood being friendly, cordial, and gracious, sharing the comforts of your home and doing your part generously], for through it some have entertained angels without knowing it."

Heb. 13:2. Amplified Version.

Sometimes God allows angels to visit you without any announcement or goose feelings. They may come to you as strangers or foreigners. They may come as travelers who just need food and lodging. You will not even know until the miracles of hosting them begin to manifest in your life and environment.

Abraham received angels in Genesis 18. He was sensitive to recognize that these were angels on assignment. They were actually on their way to Sodom. That reception by Abraham opened up the door for him to receive the long awaited miracle in less than one year. An angel is coming by your office, house and church this week or next. Your reception of them can determine whether that miracle you have been waiting for will manifest or not.

Lot lodged two angels in Genesis 19. He and his daughters were saved from the destruction that came on Sodom and Gomorrah. How many people and places have been destroyed by natural disasters just because they did not entertain the angels sent to them?

Before the Tsunami hit Asia, an angel visited one town in India. A man of God discerned him and received his message. As a result of that, their town was spared from the devastation of the Tsunami. All other towns around this particular town were badly devastated by the Tsunami.

Baby Jesus would have been killed if Joseph and Mary had not heeded the message of the angel sent to them. Think of many children who died at Herod's command in a bid to seek out the new born King Jesus. Angels may have been sent to some parents but they did not entertain the angels sent to them.

As you read this, I want you to prepare your heart to be sensitive to the angels sent to you. Your response to them can become your lifesaver from the next disaster that would hit your town or community or office or home. Save yourself untold hardship and sorrow by entertaining the angels sent on assignment to you or your community.

Putting Your Angels To Work

4

THE MINISTRY OF ANGELS

There are several rankings of angels you will find in your Bible. From my personal studies, I have placed them in four groups. These are:

One, the Archangel's. I think that there are several archangels although the Bible mentions only one named Michael. Jude 9. There is another archangel who will blow the last trumpet. 1 Thess. 4:16. These archangels are also called chief angels or elders. They are angels who have other angels under their command. So they lead other angels to carry out certain task that require more than one angel. Rev. 7:1-2. 12:7.

Two, the Cherubim's. These are mighty angelic beings. They praise, bless and adore the Most High God ceaselessly. They are ministering spirits manifesting God's invisible presence. They carry God's awesome presence and they have speed when in action. They are symbols of God's omnipotence and omnipresence in action. They literally carry the THRONE of God with wheels. Psa. 18:10. Ezek. 1 and 10.

These angels are protectors of God's interest. They are keepers and guards over God's properties. Gen. 3:24. Exo. 25:18-21. These awesome living creatures manifest the aura and life giving force of God. Rev. 4.

Three, the Seraphim's. These are the fiery or burning angels. They are the consuming flames of God. Gen. 3:24. They can consume anything but never burn out. At God's command, they can burn bushes to get the attention of people like Moses. Exo. 3:1-3. They can become walls of fire for protection. Exo. 13:21-22. They can fall on a person or place as fire balls. Judges 6:21. 1

Kings 18:24, 38. They are used by God to burn unholy things from human instruments and beings thus separating these persons to be used by God. Isa. 6:1-4.

When God calls certain men, He assigns these fiery angels for their protection because of the nature of their assignment. Elisha had them as his security guards when a king sent his army to capture this prophet. 2 Kings 6:17. I strongly believe that as I travel around the world, I need these angels to go with me into strange places and people. Quite frankly, I see their signs.

Prophet Elijah was carried away by these fiery angels when his assignment was completed. 2 Kings 2:11. I believe that when it is my time to leave a place before danger or disaster, these angels somehow will supernaturally move me out. I will never forget many times when I have escaped been stranded in strange lands. Some years ago, I just finished a meeting in Ogoni land on a Sunday morning. Normally, I would stay until the next day before taking my time to leave. But on this Sunday, I was constrained to leave that same night. Incidentally, it was that same night four Ogoni chiefs were killed. By the next day, there was a siege in land. I would have been trapped but God saved me.

When the twin towers were attacked by terrorists in New York in September 11, 2001, I can say that I escaped. I had preached at the Creekview Assembly of God Church in Amherst, New York September 2, 2001. I preached on what I titled, Lord, Send the Rain. This was autumn. The leaves were brown. While I was screaming in the church, Lord, send the rain, the heavens opened and it rained. They had not seen rain for a while before then. The people were so blessed that they persuaded me to stay and preach the next Sunday 9 September, 2001.

My ticket then was a Nigerian Airways ticket. Then, Nigerian Airways used to fly out of John F. Kennedy Airport every Tuesdays and Saturdays. I was so constrained to leave one week before September 11. Think of it, if I had not obeyed the leading of God by His angelic guide, I would have been stranded in New York that day. I will never forget. It was a strange hand moving me to leave one week before the terrorists struck. Glory to God!

I can testify to the fact that angels are working big time with me. I can tell you testimonies of divine protection as these angels work with me. Before the ADC plane crashed in 1996, I used to travel by ADC. I loved ADC. When I got to the airport that day, that flight was full. I pressed to be on that flight. I was refused. That day was my first time to travel on Bellview. Interestingly, the plane I begged to be on board did not arrive at destination.

Is it the London bombings of July 2005? I arrived London that morning. Usually, I would take the train to my destination. If I had taken the train, I would have traveled through the train station that was bombed. But God sent someone to pick me up from the airport by car. That was a human angel. For three days, I could not get in touch with my wife. My wife prayed and made frantic efforts to reach me. After three days, my wife and I connected. She was at peace that I was safe. Glory to God!

God delivered me from Hurricane Katrina as well. I got into New Orleans the day after the Mardi Gras festival ended. I am very certain that this festival must have opened up New Orleans to the devastation that Hurricane Katrina brought to New Orleans. If you know anything about this festival, it is a festival of flesh. It glorifies flesh. I left New Orleans just a few days before Katrina hit. The angel of God was at work with me moving me away from danger and destruction every step of the way.

"For he shall give his angels charge over thee, to keep thee in all thy ways.

They shall bear thee up in their hands, lest thou dash thy foot against a stone."

Psa. 91:11-12.

You need to learn to recognize the angels sent to you because you will be saved from many untold disaster.

Four, Celestial Dignities. All angelic beings fall into this group of angels. They are celestial beings because they live and operate from the heavens. Sometimes they are called stars and they have names.

"They fought from heaven; the stars in their courses fought against Sisera."

Judges 5:20.

"When the morning stars sang together, and all the sons of God shouted for joy?"

Job 38:7.

"He counts the stars and assigns each a name."

Psa. 147:4. The Message Version.

These angels have spirit bodies and each one is different from the other. 1 Cor. 15:40-41. They are great and powerful. 2 Peter 2:10-11. They are very many. Deut. 33:2. Dan. 7:9-10. Rev. 5:11-13. Luke 2:13.

Putting Your Angels To Work

5

SEVEN THINGS ANGELS DO

There are many things that angels do and can do at God's command. But I want to show you seven very important things that they do.

One, they praise, worship, bless and adore the Most High God their Maker. Heb. 1:6. Luke 2:13-14. That is what they do all the time.

Two, they wait on God to take specific instruction before they act. They don't act involuntarily. For them, there is no reflex action. Their actions are the result of their obedience to God's command. Psa. 103:19-21.

Three, they execute the judgments of God. God uses them to carry out every task that must be done on earth as far as His programs and plans are concerned for people and places. Genesis 19.

Four, they protect, watch over and guard God's interest. They watch over God's word to make it work. They watch over God's children to protect them. Not only do they protect God's children, they also provide at God's command whatever they need. They are the delivery agents of God. If God gives you the answer to your prayers or supplies for the accomplishment of His purpose in your life, angels will deliver them to you. Psa. 34:7. 91:11. Dan. 4:13,17,23. 6:22. Matt. 18:10.

Five, they dispatch God's command with speed and precision. They don't miss. If a delivery is meant for you, they will not deliver it to someone else. They will not be a second late in their delivery. Psa. 103:20.

Six, they minister for the heirs of salvation. They serve the purpose of God in the lives and world of those who have become partakers or partners with God by reason of their personal relationship with God through the person of Jesus Christ. Heb. 1:7,14. So, if you are born again, you have become a part of God. You are an heir of God through Jesus Christ. These angels are assigned to you to see that God's purpose and plan are accomplished in your life and world.

Seven, they are God's harvesters. They work on God's command to reap the harvest fields of the earth. This is why sometimes angels are involved in the salvation of people as they help in getting these people to the place or persons who will speak the message of salvation into their lives. Angels cannot preach the message of salvation. But they are important in moving people to places and people where they can hear the word that brings salvation, healing, deliverance, prosperity, lifting and life. Matt. 13:39,49. 24:31. Rev. 14:15-18.

Angels are very important in your harvest as well. When you have planted your seeds, you will need angels to help you gather your harvest from the four corners of the earth. In gathering your harvest, they sift or sever the wheat from the tares. They are so meticulous to deliver to you that which you really deserved based on the seeds you have sown. If you have sown tares, they will gather and deliver tares at your doorsteps. The seed you sow will determine the harvest they will gather and deliver at your doorsteps.

"Be not deceived; God is not mocked: for whatsoever a man soweth, that shall he also reap.

8 For he that soweth to his flesh shall of the flesh reap corruption; but he that soweth to the Spirit shall of the Spirit reap life everlasting.

9 And let us not be weary in well doing: for in due season we shall reap, if we faint not.

10 As we have therefore opportunity, let us do good unto all men, especially unto them who are of the household of faith."

Gal. 6:7-10.

Putting Your Angels To Work

6

YOU AND YOUR ANGELS

Every child of God has at least one angel assigned to them depending on the assignment each person is ordained to accomplish on earth. Some people call them guardian angels. Matthew 18:10 tells us that these little ones have angels that behold the face of God in heaven. Who are these little ones?

First, in answer to a question from His disciples, Jesus took a child He calls little one. That by implication tells us that children have an angel assigned to them.

"At the same time came the disciples unto Jesus, saying, Who is the greatest in the kingdom of heaven?

And Jesus called a little child unto him, and set him in the midst of them,

Take heed that ye despise not one of these little ones; for I say unto you, That in heaven their angels do always behold the face of my Father which is in heaven."

Matt. 18:1-2,10.

These angels have a duty to protect the children they are assigned to from danger. I believe this strongly from experience. I will never forget how I was delivered from danger and death severally as a child. While I was in elementary school, I joined some children to a pond we used to call *damba damba* at the senior staff quarters in Warri. I remember that as soon as I entered that pond to swim, a snake came after me. I could not have escaped the swift pursuit of that snake if not for the intervention of my angel.

At another time, I joined several children to the white neighborhood dumpsite that we used to call *oyibo dirty*. The white folks sent their guard dogs after us. These were Alsatian dogs well trained to hunt. I will never forget how this dog passed me while I hid behind a plant. I know that it was my angel that protected me because these dogs were trained to hunt trespassers' by smell and sight. The dog passed by me and I escaped. My angel was at work.

How can I forget when a car ran into me as a child? Then, the only tarred road in Warri was the Warri-Sapele road. Okumagba Avenue road was just completed. As a new road, this man was having a joy ride. As a child, we were not used to cars plying the road. Either I was on the road or I ran into the road when this car ran into me. My angel was at work. My life was preserved by the angel sent on assignment in my life and world. I am still alive today because my angel has been at work.

Second, Jesus used the little child as an illustration of what we look like when we believe in Him. The day you gave your life to Christ and become born again, you are like a little child. The angels rejoice that you are saved. I believe that they rejoice over you seeing that their efforts were not in vain. You know that kind of joy you experience and express when you see at last your efforts have paid off. That is the kind I think they express.

"Likewise, I say unto you, there is joy in the presence of the angels of God over one sinner that repenteth."

Luke 15:10.

When you are converted from whatever religion you are in right now to become a believer in Jesus Christ as your Lord and Savior, God assigns angels to work for you. Matt. 18:3-6,10.

What do these angels do for you now that you are a believer in Jesus Christ? One, they pitch their camp or tent around you to deliver you.

"The angel of the Lord encampeth round about them that fear him, and delivereth them."

Psa. 34:7.

One translation tells us that they mount a sentry around your life. They are on guard 24/7 to accompany, defend and preserve you in all your ways. They literally carry you through life's journey. In the water, they will be there with you to make sure that you are not drowned. I would have died some years ago at Patani river where we went swimming. I used to swim with my rubber sandals. That day, in the middle of the river, I wanted to know the depth. I dipped. When I came out, my sandals dragged me back. Usually, at the third dip, the person dies. It was after the third dip, that my cousin and his friend realized that I was drowning. They came from behind and rescued me. My angel was at work

Your angels will be at work to make sure that if you are in a fire, the fire will become comfortable for you. You will not be burned. It was this kind of fire that the Hebrew boys, Shadrach, Meshach and Abednego were thrown into by the king of Babylon. When the king and his men came to check them up the next day, they counted not just three men thrown into the fiery furnace but four. The forth one was the angel of God. This was their testimony:

"He answered and said, Lo, I see four men loose, walking in the midst of the fire, and they have no hurt; and the form of the fourth is like the Son of God." Dan. 3:25.

Your angel will preserve you from every burning fire. You shall not burn. There shall be no hurt of any kind. Your angel will deliver you when flood comes. Notice that they will not stop the flood from coming but they will deliver you from the flood. No matter the danger you find yourself in the air, water or land, they will deliver you. They have a covenant with God to deliver you as you work in collaboration with them. I have seen God's angels deliver me on mission trips to Ikpidiama after Ivrogbo in

Isokoland. That mission brought down the forces of darkness. While crossing the river, the storms came against our boat. God saved us. I can't forget our trip to Twon Brass and Okpoma some years ago. The storm that came on us left us almost without hope of survival. Everyone in the boat was drenched. Our boat almost capsized. God saved us. Angels are at work for me.

"When thou passest through the waters, I will be with thee; and through the rivers, they shall not overflow thee: when thou walkest through the fire, thou shalt not be burned; neither shall the flame kindle upon thee."

Isa. 43:2.

I know that a burning question in your mind is, if this is true, how come some people of God get killed by disasters? Yes, God has assigned these angels to work for you. They are not under your command. They are under God's command. So, they work with you as long as you obey simple instructions. In Acts 27, you will find an interesting reading of God's word to show you how this works. At one point on that journey, Paul perceived that danger was ahead. He told the captain in command. But they did not believe him. Instead of listening to Paul, they went on with the vote of the majority. Being in the majority does not make it right.

"But the centurion, instead of listening to what Paul said, followed the advice of the pilot and of the owner of the ship.

Since the harbor was unsuitable to winter in, the majority decided that we should sail on, hoping to reach Phoenix and winter there..."

Acts 27:11-12. New International Version.

After so many days of battling with the storm to save at least their lives, the angel of God told Paul that there shall be no loss of life.

"For there stood by me this night the angel of God, whose I am, and whom I serve,

Saying, Fear not, Paul; thou must be brought before Caesar: and, lo, God hath given thee all them that sail with thee."

Acts 27:23-24.

Although they lost the ship and valuables, their lives were preserved by the angel of God working with Paul. They would have been saved all the losses if they had listened to what Paul said.

"Then as they had eaten nothing for a long time, Paul came forward into their midst and said, Men, you should have listened to me, and should not have put to sea from Crete and brought on this disaster and harm and misery and loss."

Acts 27:21. Amplified Version.

"With this Message from God, your Redeemer, The Holy of Israel: "I am God, your God, who teaches you how to live right and well. I show you what to do, where to go.

If you had listened all along to what I told you, your life would have flowed full like a river, blessings rolling in like waves from the sea."

Isa. 48:17-18. THE MESSAGE.

Every time a child of God has been caught and destroyed in a flood or fire or accident, there has always been a lack of listening to the voice of God guiding us through His angels assigned to us. If Lot's wife had listened to the angels' instruction not to look back, she would have been preserved. Gen. 19:15-22, 26.

Always listen for that simple instruction and follow it. I remember when my friend was going to drop me off at the Reagan airport in Washington DC. We had no GPS. At some point we were missing our way. It was raining and I was running late to catch my flight. The men we asked for direction simply guided us to where we will see the signs. I remember them saying to us, follow the signs. Till today, those words ring in my ear: follow the signs. You can't miss your way if you follow the signs. Sometimes, we see or hear or feel the signs and we ignore them. Then, suddenly disaster strikes and we blame God or someone else.

I was listening to Dr. Mike Murdock tell the story of one of his friends who died in a plane crash. He was so devastated by it until one day while he had dinner with the man's wife. The wife told him in confidence that early that morning, her husband woke up saying to her that something tells him not to fly that day. He ignored that warning from his angel, got on his plane and crashed. He died leaving unanswered questions in many minds because he was a public figure. People will never know that he had ignored the voice of his angel and blame God for his crash which led to his death.

Two, now that you are a believer in Jesus Christ, your angels have been assigned to you to activate and actualize God's word in your life. Every word God speaks into your life or concerning your life are activated and brought to pass by angelic beings. They will take God's word and make it work in your life, marriage, business, ministry, profession, etc. Every prophetic word that has gone forth over your life will come to pass as these angels work for you.

"So bless God, you angels, ready and able to fly at his bidding, quick to hear and do what he says.

Bless God, all you armies of angels, alert to respond to whatever he wills."

Psa. 103:20-21. THE MESSAGE.

As these angels pitch their tent around your life, they wait for orders from God in collaboration with your prayers, confession and obedience to bring to pass God's word in your life. Your prayers move them to work. Your confession of your faith in God's word moves them to work. Your obedience to God's word moves them to work for you. That is why you must pray without ceasing. If you cease, they cease from working for you. That is why your confessions are powerful. If you keep saying the wrong things, you literally put them on flight safe mode.

Watch the confessions of your mouth. Speak only the right things. Speak only God's word concerning you. Your obedience is most potent. They obey God. They can't tolerate anyone who disobeys God. Your obedience moves them to work for you.

There are many believers in Christ whose angels have been so dormant that I think that they must have asked God to reassign them to some other persons or places where there is much activity. Do not let your angels' just hang out around you doing nothing. Put them to work regularly as you pray regularly, make your confessions consistently and be prompt to obey God's instructions to you.

Putting Your Angels To Work

7

PUTTING YOUR ANGELS

TO WORK

One question that people have asked consistently is, can you send angels on errands? It is a big question that many have wrestled with over the years. The answer is simple: angels answer directly to God. They were created by God for His pleasure. The creature answers to the creator. The ownership rights of angels are the exclusive privilege of God. They are His angels. They belong to Him for He made them.

"Praise ye him, all his angels: praise ye him, all his hosts. Let them praise the name of the Lord: for he commanded, and they were created."

Psa. 148:2,5.

By their name, they are messengers of God. They are God's errand boys if I may use that word. They are instruments of God's divine will. They exist to do His will. His word and His will are one and the same. So, they exist to do His word.

"So bless God, you angels, ready and able to fly at his bidding, quick to hear and do what he says. Bless God, all you armies of angels, alert to respond to whatever he wills."

Psa. 103:20-21. The Message Version.

"For he orders his angels to protect you wherever you go."

Psa. 91:11. The Living Bible.

He has given His angels orders to protect you wherever you go. That is an order that makes them loyal to human beings. By this order, before the fall of man, man was in the same class with God and a little above angels in ranking. By this order, at creation of man, God put all things that He created including angels under the authority of man.

"What is man that You are mindful of him, and the son of [earthborn] man that You care for him? Yet You have made him but a little lower than God [or heavenly beings], and You have crowned him with glory and honor. You made him to have dominion over the works of Your hands; You have put all things under his feet."

Psa. 8:4-6. Amplified Version.

Before Christ accomplished His work of redemption at the cross of Calvary after the fall of man, no human being could command angels because man had fallen below. Orders flow from the top down. Judges 13:15-16. At the cross, Jesus was still human. The price for man's redemption had not been paid. Therefore, the flow of order to angels came from God alone and directly. For any man to ask for angelic assistance, they had to pray to God who gives the orders.

"Surely you know I could ask my Father, and he would give me more than twelve armies of angels."

Matt 26:53. New Century Version.

Redeemed man was elevated to seat with Christ in heavenly places after the price for our total redemption was paid. Christ received all authority when God raised Him from the dead.

"And Jesus came and spake unto them, saying, All power is given unto me in heaven and in earth."

Matt. 28:18.

Everyone who receives Christ into his or her heart as Lord, takes the same position with Christ. In redemption, man shares the special privilege of seating with Jesus Christ, the Lord of lords and King of kings.

"And He raised us up together with Him and made us sit down together [giving us joint seating with Him] in the heavenly sphere [by virtue of our being] in Christ Jesus (the Messiah, the Anointed One)."

Eph. 2:6. Amplified Version.

By virtue of our joint seating with Christ in heavenly places, we share His authority over God's creation. So, only in Christ Jesus can a human being command angels and they obey. They obey a redeemed man in Christ because when you speak from that position, they hear you as though it is Christ Himself speaking. You speak as God's representative or ambassador.

"Then said Jesus to them again, Peace be unto you: as my Father hath sent me, even so send I you."

John 20:21.

So if you have been redeemed by the blood of Jesus Christ, the same order and authority has been given to you over angelic beings. You can speak in God's stead. You can speak in Christ name and angels will obey you. They obey you not because of anything special about you. They obey you because they think it is Christ speaking through you.

When you pray, without you knowing it, God sends angels to work for you. Your confessions of faith also become the fuel upon which the angels assigned to you run. The more you speak God's word concerning your situation, the more you accelerate the speed they ride on. Your confession put speed to their action. They watch over God's word in your mouth to make sure it works the assigned purpose.

When you have this knowledge, you will be more careful to watch what comes out of your mouth. Watch it because there are angels watching over what you speak in order to make it work. Speak faith filled words. Speak positive words over your finances, family and future. Don't keep your mouth shut if you don't want to end up shut up in prison. Speak until you see yourself free and full. Speak until you see what you speak come to pass.

"He was treated harshly, but endured it humbly;

he never said a word.

Like a lamb about to be slaughtered,

like a sheep about to be sheared,

he never said a word.

8 He was arrested and sentenced and led off to die,

and no one cared about his fate.

He was put to death for the sins of our people."

Isaiah 53:7-8. Good News Translation.

From this day, do not leave your life to chance any more. You shape your world by employing the services of God's angels assigned to you. Keep them busy. Keep them active by speaking the right words. Your angels are ready to act on God's word from your mouth. Engage them!

Putting Your Angels To Work

WHY I CHOSE JESUS CHRIST?

Someone asked me many years ago, Mike, why did you accept Jesus Christ? I could have become an atheist, a Muslim, etc. Why Jesus Christ?

My answer to that question is for basically three reasons and the fourth one will blow your mind.

One, I accepted Jesus Christ because I needed a Father. A father is a life source. That means you came from him. According to the law of sustenance, you can only be sustained by your source. Fish came out of water and thus can only be sustained in a water environment. If you put it on land, no matter how nice looking, it will die in no distant time. I realized that God is my Source. I can only be sustained by Him. I discovered that I couldn't have a personal relationship with Him through any other one or way except through Jesus Christ. John 14:6. Acts 4:12.

Like a fish out of water in a land environment, you and I continue to struggle to survive until we reconnect with our natural habitat or source. This is God your Father. This happens only through Jesus Christ. You will never be fulfilled or become eternally relevant until you accept Jesus Christ into your heart as your personal Lord and Master. Then will you be able to connect with God your Source. Then will you know what it means to be sustained by the grace of God.

Two, I accepted Jesus Christ because I needed a friend. Man was designed to relate with his environment and people. Nobody can survive as an island. You will need friends in your life. For me, it is very easy to make friends. As I grew up, my life became messed up by the friends I had. Friends betrayed me. Some battered me. Yet some others left me each time after our relationship with bruises. The marks will always be there. It was my search unknown to me for the real friend that got me into such relationships. I did not know about the Friend that sticks closer than a brother. Proverbs 18:24.

Friends have scorned me like they did Job. Job's friends turned aside from him (Job 6:18). They laughed him to scorn (Job 12:4). He was such a laughing stock that his eyes poured out tears to God (Job 16:20). His kinfolks failed him. His friends forgot him (Job 19:14). I have been there.

I needed a friend who will love me the way I am. I found this Friend in Jesus. He is God who became Abraham's Friend (Gen. 18:17. 2 Chron. 20:7). What a Friend He was to Abraham that even when Abraham lied about his wife, God rebuked the king to restore Abraham's wife (Gen. 12:10-20. 20:1-18.). A true friend will be there for you in good times and bad ones. Jesus is the best Friend I have ever had in my life. (John 15:14).

You will never know a true friend outside of Jesus Christ. Your parents? Spouse? Relatives? Classmates? Colleagues? I chose Jesus Christ because He will be there for me all the time. He said so and I believe Him.

Three, I needed a future. Life is past, present and future. I have seen the past; it was both good and bad. I cannot do anything about it. It is gone forever. I failed in the past. I did all the bad things in the past. But it is gone leaving me with the consequences of my wrong choices and deeds. Now I am in the present. What can I do to make the difference for my future? This is what I am concerned with today. I discovered that it is only in Jesus Christ that His precious blood washes my past away. My today is secured with His ever-abiding presence because He is a very present help. My tomorrow is taken care of because He told me not to worry about it.

I have a beautiful future in Jesus Christ because of what He did for me at the cross. I sinned and deserved to die. He took my sins and died in my place. In exchange, He gave me His very life, abundant life.

The fourth reason is that He changed my life. Religion tries to change people by principles, philosophies and practices. But Jesus came into my life without Him putting any demands on me to do things to earn His forgiveness. All He asked from me was to believe and receive Him. I did and found that my life is just changing every day. When I started this journey, I did not look like what I am today. I am not the same every day. I can assure you that by tomorrow I will become better. Until the day when I shall be changed permanently at the sound of the trump of God. From that point, I will put on immortality and incorruption. Sin shall never have dominion over me for all eternity. Is this not the kind of life you really desire from the deepest part of your being?

Today, my friend, you must make up your mind to receive Jesus Christ or reject Him. It is your choice. If you want to choose Jesus Christ, it is easy. Just say out loud:

Jesus, I believe You came to this world because You love me. Your love constrained You to the cross where You died for my sins. Jesus, I believe. Come into my heart today. Wash me with Your precious blood. Make me a new person whose love and passion will be for You the rest of my life on earth. Jesus, You are the Lord of my life from this day forward. Thank You for saving me in Jesus name. Amen.

If you have prayed this prayer, do write me today and I will send you some materials to help you in this journey to become all that God has designed you to be.

PARTNER WITH US

When God gives one man a vision, it will require the participation of several others to fulfill that vision. No single individual can carry out God's vision because God gives according to His size. Anyone who tries to fulfill God's vision by themselves either will get frustrated or finished off. In 1989, God told Brother Mike, *'Son, take this gospel and miracle power of the living Christ to the nations – impacting lives and destinies with the WORD.'* Since then, that word has been the driving force to reaching 30 million souls in at least 50 nations.

"And they beckoned unto their partners, which were in the other ship, that they should come and help them. And they came, and filled both the ships, so that they began to sink." Luke 5:7.

Through this message, we are beckoning on you to come alongside with us through your support and partnership. Help us reach millions around the world. Help us to fill our boat with a massive harvest. The beauty of this partnership is that when you help us, our boat and your boat will be filled. Together, we shall have a net breaking and boat sinking harvest.

Three things you CAN do to help us:

1. You can PRAY. Zech. 10:1. Acts 4:28-30. Eph. 6:18-20. Your prayers travel faster than the speed of light. You can commit to pray for us on a regular basis.

2. You can PLANT your seed of any size. Your money or material seed is the mobile force that moves the gospel from person to person and place to place. Your money or material is YOU GOing places you may not have the chance to be physically. Give generously. You can give your offering and seeds with your credit or debit card with this email address: ***amamieye@yahoo.co.uk*** through *https://www.pay.google.com* or MAWO account details:

GTBank account number 0038894924. If you are outside Nigeria, you can give through MoneyGram.com for free. GTBank accepts money through MoneyGram for free. Use it while the opportunity last.

In Nigeria, you can give by using your bank code as follows:

For offering, dial:
*bankcode*000*491+amount#

For tithes, dial: *bankcode*000*492+amount#

If you are using GTBank for instance, your bank code is 737, so you can dial:
*737*000*491+amount#

If you are in the United States of America, you can give your offering to Bank of America account number 0905418443. ABA Routing number is: 121000358.

With Zelle, send to: **amamieye@yahoo.co.uk**

If you are in the United Kingdom, you can give your offering to NatWest Bank account number 52344819. Sort code 602112.

3. You can PARTICIPATE with us as you join forces with us in any location near you. I look forward to see you as we gather together a net breaking and boat sinking harvest. Luke 5:7. If you hear a voice saying, ignore this message, just know that it is the old serpent from the Garden. Tell that voice to shut up because you are the sheep of Jesus and you only obey the voice of your Master Jesus Christ. John 10:27. Thank you very much for obeying His voice in your heart and for being a part of what God is doing with us around the nations.

Putting Your Angels To Work

FOR MORE INFORMATION

Send in your testimonies to let us know how this devotional has been a blessing to you.

Send in your prayer requests as well.

Stand with us to help us reach thirty million souls in fifty nations.

For more spiritual help, counseling and prayer ministration, contact:

**Bishop Michael O. Amamieye
Michael Amamieye Word Outreach,
International**

**a/k/a Aggressive Faith Ministries
Plot 13 Walter Akpana Lay Out off 394
Ikwerre Road, Mile 5 Rumueprikom, P. O.
Box 12378, Port Harcourt, Nigeria.**

**Hotlines: +234901800MAWO,
+2348050987377
WhatsApp: +2348036732188
U.S.A: +19162456157
www.aggressivefaith.org
E-mail: info@aggressivefaith.org**

Putting Your Angels To Work

ABOUT THE AUTHOR

Psalm 40:2,3 is a keynote to the life and ministry of Michael O. Amamieye. He was radically saved, healed and delivered from the power of darkness that endangered his youth. He is a living proof of God's matchless and abundant grace.

Since 1983, Brother Mike has been president, pastor and pioneer of several fellowships, churches and movements. He is instrumental in birthing many sons and daughters unto glory. He is a consecrated bishop with an oversight that reaches five continents.

In 1984, the Lord called Brother Mike to world evangelism with a mandate to *take the gospel and miracle power of the risen Christ to the nations – impacting lives and destinies with the WORD!* He is the President of **Michael Amamieye Word Outreach International** *also known as* **Aggressive Faith Ministries** with headquarters in the Garden City of Port Harcourt, Nigeria. He is the President of **Intensive Ministers Training School**. He is the Chairman of **Aggressive Faith Publishing Company**. Through this ministry, Brother Mike is determined to reach at least thirty million souls in at least fifty nations with the simple proclamation of the gospel of Christ with evidence that brings salvation, healing, deliverance, blessing and joy.

An evangelist by calling, he is a graduate of the **Billy Graham School of Evangelism**. He is a member of **Proclamation Evangelism Network** and an associate evangelist with the **Global Network of Evangelists** founded by the **Luis Palau Association**. He has been interviewed on **Decision Today** Radio broadcast and **Decision** magazine both of which are owned by the **Billy Graham Evangelistic Association.** He has also appeared on GODTV as well as several other networks around the world.

Bishop Mike is a member of the **International Communion of Charismatic Churches** founded by the late Archbishop Benson Idahosa and several others. He has been honored in a public ceremony where the Mayor of the city of East Cleveland, Ohio gave him the key to the city in 2003. **LEADS Africa** honored him as an icon of nation building in 2012. **The Voice** magazine in Holland honored him with the spiritual leadership award in 2014. In 2019, he was awarded an honorary doctorate degree by **Triune Biblical University** in New York. He is on high demand in crusades, conferences and conventions around the world.

He is the author of more than twenty books. He is a prolific and thought captivating writer with many of his works published in newsletters, magazines and newspapers around the world.

Bishop Mike is happily married to Princess Monivi, an ordained minister of the gospel and a health consultant. They are blessed with two biological children,

Edwina Aleme and Mehetabel Favour as well as many others.

Putting Your Angels To Work

Welcome To The Partner Family

"They signaled to their partners in other boat to come and take hold with them. And they came and filled both the boats, so that they began to sink." Luke 5:7. (Amplified Version).

Since the Lord gave me the vision of a massive harvest of souls through the mandate to reach 30 million souls for whom Christ died in at least 50 countries, I have not ceased to signal my partners *to come and take hold with me*.

Through our mass evangelistic crusades, we are seeing many become born again. It is amazing as God is giving us the gates of our enemies. We are seeing hardened criminals, cult leaders, gang leaders, etc, become born again.

This is possible because of the sacrifices of committed partners who have responded to our calls.

Now, it is your turn to respond to my signal. I want to give you an opportunity to fill your boat with miracles until it begins to sink.

Please check appropriate boxes:

☐ **I WANT TO BECOME A MONTHLY PARTNER.** I am expecting my partner information packet with more details. My offering is enclosed to start my partnership. I am willing to commit monthly: ☐ **$15** ☐ **$20** ☐ **$25** ☐ **$50** ☐ **$100**

☐ **I WANT TO HELP SPONSOR A CRUSADE.** Enclosed is my special one-time gift of: ☐ **$1000** ☐ **$2000** ☐ **$3000** ☐ **$__________**

**Tear this form and send to us with your prayer requests.
Use the address you find in this book.**